Detlev Foth

No Looking Back

A Play in Ten Acts

Translated by Amélie Fujiwara-Golitz

I am grateful to Amélie Fujiwara-Golitz who put this play into English and to Katherine Huhn Franklin for her wonderful support and help in proofreading.

Published by
Books on Demand GmbH
Norderstedt
ISBN: 978-3-8423-6064-8

No Looking Back

CAST

MANHOLD	sales promotion photographer
IRA	Manhold's wife, former model
LYAMAN	au-pair girl
LAURENZ	businessman
EVI	Laurenz' wife, teacher

ACT ONE

A living room, two sofas – white, a large table. You can hear a shower in the background; somebody is busy in the kitchen. The doorbell rings.

IRA: Lyaman, can you answer the door? It must be them. I'm still taking a shower. Just ask them to come in and get Manhold.

Lyaman crosses the living room and goes to the door which is not visible; a little later she shows the guests to the living room.

LYAMAN: Take a seat, please, I'll go and get the master.

LAURENZ: Your German is fantastic!

EVI: Yes, indeed!

LYAMAN: Sure, I know.

Laurenz clears his throat, Evi, feels uncomfortable, glances sideways. Lyaman leaves, Manhold enters the living room.

MANHOLD: Evi! Laurenz! How nice!

He welcomes them, embracing both.

MANHOLD: We have been meaning to do this for ages and now, finally, it has worked out. Won't you take off your coats? Do take a seat, please, make yourself at home!

EVI: Nice place you've got.

LAURENZ: Agreed, nice, just nice.

MANHOLD: Ira does this, the furniture and arrangements, everything. I used to almost live in the studio. There was no privacy; cultivated home decor was a foreign concept! Coziness: Nada, nothing!

EVI: How exciting, to know also the other way of life, the unconventional one, so to say.

MANHOLD: It was boring, all those thick models, all those powdered boobs, always those high heels, you stop looking; anyway, we made pots of money.

Evi laughs in an edgy way, Laurenz laughs a bit too loudly. With a big show Manhold buckles down on one of the sofas and lights a cigarette. Evi and Laurenz sit down on the outer edge of the other sofa; they sit side by side like passengers in a bus.

LAURENZ: Your au-pair, where is she from, by the way?

MANHOLD: Lyaman, she is from Azerbaijan.

EVI: Oh!

MANHOLD: Twenty years old, speaks fluent
           German, English, Russian and Turkish,
           makes you feel like a hillbilly
           sometimes. But me, I just need
           English, if at all.

LAURENZ: And what does she do?

MANHOLD: She is studying something; you'd better
           ask her yourself. She's told us once,
           but I've forgotten.

EVI: And how does it work out?

MANHOLD: The kid adores her.

EVI: Don't you feel hemmed in? To have a
           stranger in the house all the time, not
           everybody cares for that...

MANHOLD: Heavens, we've got nothing to hide...

EVI: Well, but one's private sphere...

MANHOLD: What's that?

*Laughs hysterically all of a sudden. Laurenz looks at him
askance. Evi giggles shrilly. Ira enters at this moment, she is
dressed provokingly.*

MANHOLD:	Ira, honey, Evi and Laurenz have already come!
IRA:	Here you are!

She embraces them. Then she sits down next to Manhold and pulls up her knees.

IRA:	Lyaman? Will you get us something to drink? We are gagging for a drink!
EVI:	Now that's a real help, an au-pair.
IRA:	Why don't you get yourself one as well? I'd really recommend it.
EVI:	But we don't have any kids.
IRA:	So what, no need to stick to the rules too closely.
MANHOLD:	Right you are.
EVI:	We wouldn't have any use for an au-pair girl.
LAURENZ:	You never know!
EVI:	Laurenz!

Lyaman carries a tray with glasses. She puts them on the table and fetches a carafe of wine.

MANHOLD: She's already decanted it, she's learning
             fast. Considering her background,
             you've got to give her credit.

Suddenly Evi sniffs something.

EVI: What a tasty aroma; you really needn't
             have taken so much trouble. We didn't
             know; we've had dinner already....

Manhold and Ira look at each other.

MANHOLD: Oh, is that so?

EVI: Yes, sure.

MANHOLD: In that case, let's pass over right away
             to the comfy part of the evening.

LYAMAN: It's not my fault that there is still a
             whiff of the roast.

IRA: Lyaman, please, nobody has asked
             you…

MANHOLD: Sometimes she gets things mixed up,
             so what, I'd say: to our health!
             Bottoms up!

IRA: Cheers, my dears.

EVI: À votre santé!

LAURENZ: Wow, here comes the schoolmistress!

EVI: Laurenz!

The four of them drink.

LAURENZ: That was good.

EVI: Yes, a good wine.

IRA: I had thought of something different.
              They do talk you into things, you never
              get the wine you actually fancy.

MANHOLD: As long as it gets you loaded.

EVI: I beg your pardon?

MANHOLD: We used to say, the main thing is that
              it creeps up on you fast.

EVI: I don't quite get you…

LAURENZ: Evi!

MANHOLD: Doesn't matter.

IRA: Past is past.

MANHOLD: So, how's business?

LAURENZ: I've retired.

MANHOLD: Really?

LAURENZ: Yes, the company bored me stiff.

MANHOLD: Oh!

EVI: One has got to set priorities.

IRA: Yes, that's true.

LAURENZ: Life is short.

MANHOLD: That's what they say.

EVI: We don't depend on the company;
             we've got my salary, too.

MANHOLD: What was it again you are teaching?

EVI: Am…

LAURENZ: Nobody gives a hoot for that…

EVI: But..

MANHOLD: It's a hard work for a poor squirrel…

EVI: I beg your pardon?

IRA: Does anyone care for some more?
             Lyaman, could you fill up, please?

MANHOLD: And what do you do now?

LAURENZ: I write, I write books, novels.

MANHOLD: Oh!

EVI: Yes, that's what he does now.

IRA: I haven't read a book for ages.

MANHOLD: Books. Well, why not!

LAURENZ: It takes all my strength.

MANHOLD: Gosh!

IRA: Perhaps I should have a read again,
             who knows what it's good for.

EVI: You needn't stress this writing too
             much; Laurenz writes to compensate
             for…

LAURENZ: Nonsense…

MANHOLD: To compensate for?

LAURENZ: No, no, I write because I've always
             been keen on literature.

MANHOLD: When I was young, I sometimes read,
             too.

IRA: I didn't.

EVI: Laurenz writes in order to…

LAURENZ:	Evi, please…
MANHOLD:	We won't sort this out anymore tonight…
IRA:	Why not?
MANHOLD:	Ira, leave well alone…
EVI:	Such a beautiful home!
MANHOLD:	Heavens, yes, yes.
IRA:	Way too small, we could hardly put up Lyaman…
MANHOLD:	She's got two rooms and a bathroom.
IRA:	But no internet access.
EVI:	That would be far too stressful for me, a stranger in one's own home.
IRA:	Lyaman, where on earth are you?

Lyaman brings along another carafe. Laurenz regards her as if he wanted to strip her. Manhold scratches his chest under the shirt; Ira clears her throat and shows off her legs, Evi blows her nose in an exaggerated way.

MANHOLD:	To a wonderful night!
IRA:	That's it!

MANHOLD:	We won't get together this young anymore.
EVI:	Time passes so fast!
LAURENZ:	Lifetime!
EVI:	Will you stop that!
MANHOLD:	The night is still young!
IRA:	As young as Lyaman…
MANHOLD:	As young as Lyaman!
EVI:	Can you tell me where the bathroom is, please?
MANHOLD:	Over there, the third door on your left.
IRA:	Cheers!
LAURENZ:	Ass is mossy.
MANHOLD:	That's a good one!
EVI:	Here we go again!

Evi leaves the living room. Manhold, Ira and Laurenz are sitting on the sofas in silence. Lyaman walks to and fro, on and off she moves the glasses.

ACT TWO

Evi comes back. She sits down on the sofa next to Laurenz.

MANHOLD: Now isn't this nice.

EVI: What exactly?

MANHOLD: That we are all so relaxed.

LAURENZ: I'm not; my novel has come to a halt, my writing stagnates. I'd like to know if I've come to live in a parallel world. Life as it is, maybe I have no idea about it.

MANHOLD: We all live in a parallel world. That doesn't mean that the release gets jammed when I take pictures.

IRA: You haven't taken pictures for ages.

MANHOLD: Don't you start that again. I've got 20,000 pictures in my archive. I still get royalties for them; I needn't stir a finger, works all by itself.

IRA: And they keep getting less. Nowadays you can buy photo rights for as little as fifty cents.

MANHOLD: Out of question in the old days.

IRA: The old days, the old days, how I hate
             this. When you talk I always think it's
             déjà-vu all over again.

MANHOLD: What are you going on about again!

IRA: Living a life of luxury, that's what it
             was in the old days.

MANHOLD: And what was bad about that?

IRA: No set was too small, you paid the
             entire crew. All those flights to Miami,
             any silly bird that could do a make-up
             like a school girl had to come along on
             the big trip.

MANHOLD: Big is better!

IRA: Ever since we've married everything
             has been going downhill…

MANHOLD: Alright, so let's get divorced, maybe
             then things will be looking up again…

LAURENZ: You 've been joking, haven't you?

Manhold and Ira smile, but say nothing.

LAURENZ: Do you call that a joke?

EVI: One shouldn't make fun of that sort of thing.

The four of them fall silent. After a long while:

MANHOLD: Lyaman!

She comes running.

MANHOLD: Lyaman, you needn't hide all the time. I know we are excessively tolerant; we don't want to have these silly role relationships here. After all, we are not those bourgeois who normally take on au-pairs to have their Porsches washed by these young chicks, to put it that way, guys who are playing the big shot, who want to do some teaching and preaching and in the end sell it as cultural exchange.

LYAMAN: What are you trying to tell me?

MANHOLD: Good heavens, isn't she cute?

IRA: My husband is trying to tell you to simply join us, not to be so formal. We are all a big family.

Lyaman sits down on the sofa next to Manhold and looks at her shoes.

MANHOLD: Lyaman, Laurenz and Evi asked me what exactly you were studying. I couldn't remember.

LYAMAN, *quick as a shot*: I am studying at the faculty of Business Administration at the Azerbaijan State Economics University.

IRA: In German! We are in Germany.

MANHOLD: Now you know. Azerbaijan is training young people who can show us how to get out of the crisis. I'll be jiggered!

IRA: Racist!

MANHOLD: Honey, you've really lost your sense of humour. Have a laugh. This was funny, wasn't it?

EVI: And what do you plan to do later?

LYAMAN: Climb the corporate ladder.

EVI: Ah, how interesting.

LAURENZ: Somebody ought to tell her.

MANHOLD: Let her dream on, she'll wake up soon enough.

LYAMAN: I must get back to the kitchen.

IRA: Now you just stay sitting here. There is
                nothing more to do in the kitchen.

MANHOLD: Yes, just stay, we won't bite.

LAURENZ: Could be a subject, a girl form
                Azerbaijan.

MANHOLD: A girl from Azerbaijan and what of it?

LAURENZ: I would have to think about that.

MANHOLD: I guess it's as dull as dishwater, a girl
                form Azerbaijan, so what? A girl from
                Azerbaijan turns up, wants to do
                business, realizes there is no business
                to do, because Germany is on its last
                legs, then she goes home again. She
                returns home empty-handed. So she is
                home and is richer by some experience
                and that's it. Of course there has also
                been no Prince Charming. That's the
                way it is, let's not pretend otherwise.
                Nobody would want to read such a
                novel. Why not write a murder
                mystery, dear Laurenz?

LAURENZ: Definitely not.

MANHOLD: And why not?

LAURENZ: That's too boorish for my taste.

MANHOLD:	There are murder mysteries which are actually well written.
IRA:	Thrilling, that is.

Ira yawns and looks at her painted fingernails.

LAURENZ:	I don't care for suspense, it's about the Truth.
EVI:	So the Truth is always without suspense or what do you want to say?
LAURENZ:	No wonder you are stabbing me in the back, I hadn't expected otherwise. Someone like me cannot expect otherwise from you.
MANHOLD:	By the way, Evi, how do you like Laurenz' books?
EVI:	Frankly speaking?
MANHOLD:	Sure, frankly speaking…
EVI:	I keep asking myself whatever does he want to say…
LAURENZ:	Evi, now really…
EVI:	And, above all, who does he want to tell his?

LAURENZ: The people out there.

MANHOLD: It's like this: the people out there want
             naked flesh again and again– and sex
             sells, nobody knows this better than
             me who's made lots of money with it.
             Let me tell you, the murder mystery as
             such is up and coming; *The Perfume*
             was also a murder mystery, you see!

IRA: But you haven't read *The Perfume* at all.

MANHOLD: I haven't, but I've seen the film, I
             guess the book won't be much
             different.

EVI: There are many who write but few are
             chosen to do so.

LAURENZ: Say whatever you like, I'll go on
             writing, time is running out for me, my
             lifetime.

EVI: He keeps talking about lifetime.

MANHOLD: Lifetime! Time to live!

EVI: Sorry?

MANHOLD: Grab what you can get hold of, take a
             chance, and don't miss out anything!
             You can take a rest once you are dead.

IRA: If that's so, you have been dead a long
            time.

MANHOLD: We'd rather listen to what our young
            guest here has to say to this,
            mysterious Lyaman who is inspiring
            Laurenz to write a new book.

Lyaman is silent and looks around in a bored way.

MANHOLD: She'll think to herself, heavens, these
            old geezers do keep on about things, a
            heap of luxury problems they've got.
            Back home they use teabags three
            times, they chat maybe ten words a
            month with each other and every
            second sentence is about whether the
            next day there'll be less or more rain
            than today. Back home where Today is
            dogged and stifling, like an eternal
            midday break, where there is nothing
            and where nothing will come, not in
            the afternoon and not in the evening
            or at night, let alone the next day. Zest
            for life just looks different I'd say;
            Lyaman knows what I'm talking about,
            she wouldn't be here, so far from
            home, if she didn't.

IRA: Here you go again, this arrogance of
            yours has made me sick ever so often.

MANHOLD:	She's hinting at my grandfather again, from the mother's side. He used to have quite a position with the Nazis, but this has got nothing at all to do with me. They say he fell in the war, but he didn't, they blew him up. Well, what a way to go! The Resistance blew him up, the barracks, the comrades, as I've said, they blew up all and everything. We can't say this about us when we drool away one day; there isn't even resistance against us, there is nothing against us, nothing but indifference.
IRA:	It's the genes, I'm telling you.
MANHOLD:	There are no Nazi genes.
IRA:	You never know.
LAURENZ:	Interesting idea.
MANHOLD:	Rubbish.
EVI:	Let's leave the past alone. We are a different kind of Germans. New Germans, completely different.
MANHOLD:	As soon as you have a critical look at a foreigner you are called a Nazi straight away.

IRA:	Patronizing, that's your way.
MANHOLD:	Nobody is looking down on anybody here, isn't that right, Lyaman?
LYAMAN:	Sorry? I haven't been listening.
MANHOLD:	You haven't missed a thing, kid.
IRA:	Shall we dance? We are sitting around here like in a nursing home.
MANHOLD:	Dance?
IRA:	Yes, dance!
MANHOLD:	We've got no music.
IRA:	Lyaman, pick a CD, any will do, as long as it's music.
EVI:	I'd rather not dance now.
LAURENZ:	I can't dance, even if I wanted to.
MANHOLD:	Ira is always on about dancing. It's been like this all the time, once she runs out of ideas she wants to dance.

There is music; it is Buena Vista Social Club.

MANHOLD:	Of all things! What've got to do with Cuba?

EVI: The film was good, though!

LAURENZ: I think Wenders is a fake.

MANHOLD: I don't like Wenders. I don't get his films, I keep falling asleep when I watch a film by Wenders. My number one favourite film is *BLOW-UP*.

IRA: A sentimental film, as old as the hills and stupid, no wonder that Hemmings got so awfully fat later. It's because he was ashamed of his photographer's trash as a role.

MANHOLD: What a film! A milestone in the history of films! Antonioni! What a director! A giant!

IRA: A flimsy plot, terribly pathetic!

EVI: I don't know the film at all.

LAURENZ: I've heard of it, but I can't get any pictures of it in my mind.

EVI: How could you, if you've only heard of it…?

IRA: I'll dance now! Is anybody joining me? Nobody? But I'll dance, I'll dance

alone then. Lyaman, won't at least you
dance? After all, where you come from
they dance all day long!

*Nobody makes a move, everyone stays seated on the sofas. Ira gets
up and dances. Lyaman gets up first, but sits down again.*

ACT THREE

*Ira, exhausted, flings herself onto the sofa next to Laurenz and
Evi.*

LAURENZ: That was a nice dance.

IRA: Come off it!

EVI: It was, it really was, takes a bit to be
              this open, to dance just like that in
              front of everybody!

IRA: I was open once, I haven't been for a
              long time.

MANHOLD: If we are anything at all, Ira, then we
              are open.

LAURENZ: More open than we are.

EVI: It's also because of my school that I
              couldn't really do what I feel like.

MANHOLD: Let's have an example; what is it you
              couldn't do?

EVI: I can't think of anything off the top of
              my head.

MANHOLD: Having photos taken of you in the nude?

LAURENZ: Who'd want the see them?

MANHOLD: Evi is an attractive woman, after all! Tell me, Evi, what would the Principal say to that?

IRA: What's the point of this crap?

EVI: He would disapprove, to say the least.

LAURENZ: What about the right to express yourself?

EVI: Laurenz, what is this, one of your constructs?

LAURENZ: I believe I've heard about that sometime...

MANHOLD: Me too; they called it something different, can't recall what it was.

IRA: A teacher is not supposed to have her photo taken in the nude, except if the pictures are solely meant for the family album.

MANHOLD: So what are you permitted to do as teacher?

EVI: I'm supposed to set a good example.

MANHOLD: I see.

EVI: Yes, I am.

MANHOLD: But in this private relationship you
                would be allowed to strip and set a
                good example for us, wouldn't you?

*Laurenz laughs, Evi kneads her hands nervously, Lyaman starts
                listening.*

EVI: Why should I do that?

IRA: Haven't you seen enough naked
                women in all these years, Manhold?
                Can't you get enough?

MANHOLD: Suppose I wanted to see Evi?

LAURENZ: Yes, suppose he wanted to see Evi!

EVI: You don't want to see me, but this is
                turning you, I don't know what this is
                turning you into…

MANHOLD: I just put myself into Manhold's shoes,
                that's all.

EVI: You are making fun of me, all of you,
                at my expense.

MANHOLD: Nobody is making fun of you, believe me, I'm serious; show us that a teacher can be easy going, too.

EVI: I know a lot of male and female teachers who are easy going without stripping.

MANHOLD: Alright, let's drop it.

Manhold paces up and down. The others stare into space, then look down on the floor.

MANHOLD: Let me tell you frankly, in the old days Ira and me didn't waste any opportunity, but once you are in your mid-forties everything seems to change. I have been warned time and again, but I have never believed it.

LAURENZ: What do you mean you didn't waste any opportunity?

MANHOLD: We've been to lots of parties, we've hardly missed one. And I'm not talking about parties where you hang around nibbling pretzels.

LAURENZ: We've also been to some parties.

MANHOLD: So?

LAURENZ: So what?

IRA: Manhold, will you stop it.

MANHOLD: Ira, come on, why not tell about our
            parties.

IRA: Who cares to hear about that!

EVI: We want to.

LAURENZ: Yes, we want to hear.

IRA: I'm sure you won't want to hear about
            that.

MANHOLD: Perhaps Lyaman cares to hear
            something, Lyaman, do you have
            parties back home?

LYAMAN: We do, when someone is celebrating a
            birthday.

*Manhold gives a brief laugh. He stands at a window which
cannot be seen. Ira uncovers her right shoulder, Laurenz dabs
sweat off his forehead with a handkerchief.*

MANHOLD: So that's what it's like to get old.

LAURENZ: You aren't old. None of us is old! Are
            we old? I definitely don't think we are
            old.

IRA:	We are definitely not young any more.
EVI:	You are as old as you feel.
MANHOLD:	My God!
EVI:	It's not as if we didn't do anything at all. We've also had a time of experiments.
MANHOLD:	How am I to understand this?
EVI:	Like so many couples who want to broaden their minds, it's a long time ago and I'm only telling you so that you won't get any wrong ideas about us, after all we are not as square as you might think.
MANHOLD:	Do the two of you think we are attractive, as couple?
IRA:	What a question!
MANHOLD:	No, really, I want to know.
EVI:	You both are interesting.
MANHOLD:	A coffee-table book on Mongolia is interesting.
LAURENZ:	One should define what exactly

attraction is supposed to mean.

MANHOLD: Lyaman, do you think Ira and I are attractive?

LYAMAN: Yes, I do.

Manhold turns around and looks at Lyaman with glassy eyes.

IRA: What else is she supposed to say!

MANHOLD: Would a couple like Ira and me be an attractive couple back at your home, too?

LYAMAN: For each other?

MANHOLD: No, for others.

LYAMAN: But for whom, if not for each other?

EVI: Smart counter question!

LAURENZ: She didn't get the point.

MANHOLD: Of course she didn't get it.

IRA: Nobody gets it.

MANHOLD: Ira, come off it! Just once, be like in the old days!

IRA: I behave the way I do, because I am

the way I am now.

MANHOLD: And which way are you now?

IRA: Different

MANHOLD: Laurenz, would you like a Cialis?

LAURENZ: What for?

MANHOLD: Just for fun, as a test. Let me tell you, they work wonders.

IRA: Sure, you go and get your Cealis, and then we'll see what happens.

LAURENZ: What's going to happen, then?

MANHOLD: We'll see.

EVI: One shouldn't fool about with drugs. Besides, we've had alcohol.

MAHOLD: Lyaman, go and fetch the Cialis.

IRA: Lyaman is not going to get anything; you go and get them yourself, your Cialis.

Manhold leaves and returns with a bag full of loose pills. He bangs the bag onto the table.

MANHOLD: There you are, from the internet.

Laurenz, help yourself. The stuff has been cut, so have two or three.

LAURENZ: I'm not quite sure what your point is in doing this.

MANHOLD: I'll tell you later.

LAURENZ: Come on, tell me.

MANHOLD: The point is: things that work wonders don't work on us, because we don't believe in miracles anymore.

IRA: He's on about having one of his sex parties again. They have always been total flops.

MANHOLD: I don't want a sex party, I just want to demonstrate something.

Laurenz determinedly takes two pills; Evi looks at her watch, Lyaman aspirates covertly into her hand to check if she has got bad breath. Manhold paces back and forth as before. Ira is fanning air with her hand.

IRA: Aren't you hot, too? Maybe it's the heavy wine.

LAURENZ: I don't feel a thing!

MANHOLD: How should you! You have to wait for

another half hour.

LAURENZ: And then?

MANHOLD: We'll see.

EVI: Bizarre!

MANHOLD: What did you say?

EVI: All this is so bizarre!

LYAMAN: I'd better check on the boy…

MANHOLD: The boy is fast asleep, you needn't go
and look after him; simply relax or are
you bored being with us?

LYAMAN: No, no, I'm not.

MAHOLD: There.

IRA: I'm incredibly hot, aren't you, too?

Evi, Laurenz and Lyaman look blank at her. Manhold lights a cigarette. Ira brushes her hair away from her face and crosses her arms behind her head.

ACT FOUR

They sit on the sofas, no change in posture. Manhold has sat down, too.

MANHOLD: So what's left after all? If business isn't doing well any more, what's left then? There is still this something that used to urge you on in the old days, you are just older now.

IRA: Manhold never had to chase after success. Success came to him.

MANHOLD: And then suddenly it was over. One or two major customers, who used to book you for years and years dropped out. I never bothered with small customers, never even answered their inquiries. First you got the digital flood, then the recession; it's as simple as that. Now I'm worse off than twenty years ago. I've even been thinking of changing to artistic photography…

IRA: You are no artist.

MANHOLD: Can't be that hard.

IRA: You are an advertising photographer, not an artist.

MANHOLD: There is nothing left I could do any advertising for.

LAURENZ: And what's motivating you?

MANHOLD: Nothing motivates me.

LAURENZ: But you did say that there is something
            that urges you on, something that used
            to urge you on in the old days…

MANHOLD: Really? Did I say so?

IRA: Yes, you did say so. I'd also love to
            know what that could be that's driving
            you.

MANHOLD: I've forgotten what's urging me on.
            What about you all? What's driving
            you?
            What is it that's driving Lyaman? What
            motivates people?

IRA: Questions, questions, it's always
            questions; for me, it's first of all about
            surviving this crisis.

MANHOLD: That's what it's all about these days:
            that all things ended up in a crisis.

EVI: Can't you shift paths a little? Job wise,
            I mean, away from photography, I'd
            think.

MANHOLD: At the age of forty-five?

LAURENZ: Impossible. At that age inconceivable, totally unrealistic.
The financial crisis turned me from a director into a nobody. My company went bankrupt because of the crisis; it would still exist if it weren't for the downturn.
Now it has gone, it is no longer; my father's work is now a mountain of debts which I cannot ever repay.

EVI: We are living off my money.

LAURENZ: I'm a guest in Evi's house. I'm sponging off her; with the debts in my mind's eye, I feel like a drip, a nonety. The books are no help.

EVI: You can write, but you aren't an artist. You are not an artist just because it suits your plans.

MANHOLD: Let's stop moping around. So we do have debts and we happen to be no artists. Anyway, I've never really understood artists, for me, they always come across as, how should I say, simply like from another planet. Laurenz, you just keep writing your books, if they boost your ego ; financially speaking there won't be much of a boost, I guess…

LAURENZ: It's not for money that I'm writing.

EVI: The gentleman has no need of that…

MANHOLD: All the better, no, I mean it, go on writing; what else should you do with time on your hand…?

IRA: And what do you do with your time?

MANHOLD: I'm waiting.

IRA: Yes, I can see that.

Manhold jumps up and shouts:

MANHOLD: And you, Ira, what do you do?

IRA: I won't go into that, not when I'm spoken to like this.

Manhold pops down onto the sofa again.

MANHOLD: Alright then, let's face the crash, so
             there are debts; the debts grow and
             grow and – what happens then
             actually? I've never thought about that.
             I'm almost like those artists, they never
             think about that sort of thing either…

IRA: Because they think about other things,
             different from you. You don't give a
             thought about anything.

MANHOLD: In the old days, when I made money
             without any hassle, lots of money,
             outrageous amounts of money, I was
             much in demand, also by Ira, but now,
             when I need her, she complains, she
             shows her total contempt for me, she
             who was never shy to spend my
             money.

IRA: It's because I'm afraid, that's all.

MANHOLD: Afraid?

IRA: Yes, afraid.

MANHOLD: Lyaman, they say that in your place
             there are poor people. Are they afraid?

LYAMAN: We trust in fate.

MANHOLD: There you are! We should do that, too,
             trust in fate.

IRA:	Fate has been kind to you once; do you really think there is a second time, after having taken the first time for granted?
LAURENZ:	People do learn from mistakes.
IRA:	Manhold doesn't.
EVI:	Even Manhold does.
MANHOLD:	Tell you one thing: all this makes me so sick.
IRA:	You are not the only one.

Manhold gets up again and paces restlessly around in the room. Laurenz gets up, too and walks to and fro.

IRA:	Now they have run out of ideas.
EVI:	We ought to turn to some other thoughts.
IRA:	Should we?
EVI:	Anything else is destructive.
IRA:	You think so?
EVI:	Yes, I do. There is no point in this. You need to be constructive, that's what I keep telling my students.

IRA: Really? So, let's be constructive.

EVI: Exactly.

IRA: You go ahead then.

EVI: I will.

Both of them stay seated. Ira stares at Evi, and then heaves a moaning disgustedly.

LAURENZ: Those Cialis of yours are fakes.

MANHOLD: Definitely not, I've already tested
                them.

LAURENZ: Together with Ira?

MANHOLD: With Ira.

IRA: With me? When should have that
                been?

MANHOLD: The other day.

IRA: You've tested them all by yourself,
                definitely not together with me.

MANHOLD: Anyway, I know Cialis works and
                that's what this is all about, nothing
                else.

LAURENZ: But shouldn't I start feeling some sort
                of effect.

MANHOLD: Without stimulation the effect goes up
              in smoke, of course, so this pill is like
              all things in life.

*Ira gets up and walks over to Laurenz in the affected style of the
model she used to be. She runs her hand over his chest down to
the buckle of his belt. She smirks. Laurenz turns pale.*

IRA: Evi said we should be constructive, so
              that's what I'm now. And you,
              Laurenz, do you feel something, am I
              stimulating enough?

LAURENZ: This is now asking too much of me.

MANHOLD: Real easy to overstrain you.

EVI: He's always been like this.

MANHOLD: So?

LAURENZ: So what?

MANHOLD: Fakes, you said?

IRA: Manhold, why didn't you take any
              Cialis? After all, you feel so positive
              about them.

MANHOLD: And then I'd be standing around, all
              excited, making a fool of myself, right?
              You would like that; I know how
              much you'd like that.

IRA: You have some, too; be at least that
            fair to Laurenz.

MANHOLD: Alright, I'll have some as well; you'll
            have to answer for this.

IRA: Okay, okay, I'll answer for this.

EVI: I guess we should be going home.

MANHOLD: No, don't, the evening has only just
            started.

IRA: Have some!

MANHOLD: I will, for sure.

IRA: Lyaman, please go and get two pills
            and some water.

Lyaman does as requested and hands all to Manhold.

MANHOLD: Now you look her, I'm swallowing the
            stuff, but I won't answer for anything,
            that's for sure.

IRA: No need to get ceremonial, what's
            going to happen anyway? Nothing is
            going to happen, it's all fantasy.

MANHOLD: You can imagine lots of things, but the
            effect of Cialis is definitely not an
            illusion.

47

LAURENZ:	I can feel my pulse quicken, that's all.
MANHOLD:	Can't be, that happens only with Viagra.
IRA:	Here comes the expert.
EVI:	Where is this going to lead to? We'd rather continue this evening at a later date.
MANHOLD:	Used to do anything, used to do anything with anybody, lived through it all, saw it all, enjoyed life to the full, also Ira, and now this: We behave like students in a youth hostel who are afraid that the police will show up. Actually we are all grown-up, free people, aren't we?
EVI:	And because I'm grown-up and free I'd rather go home.
LAURENZ:	Go home then; I'll stay.
EVI:	All by yourself? This is really news.
LAURENZ:	I will stay.
MANHOLD:	Laurenz is staying, didn't you hear, Evi?

IRA:	Please, do stay, Evi.
EVI:	I've got to get up early tomorrow morning.
LAURENZ:	It's Sunday tomorrow, no need for you to get up early.
EVI:	Oh, right, tomorrow is Sunday.
LYAMAN:	I'm going to bed.
IRA:	Lyaman, we've got guests, one cannot just go to bed then and you can't either.
LYAMAN:	And what am I supposed to do?
IRA:	Nothing. You are always on about having to do something. Are we doing anything? Is it so difficult to open yourself to a situation, to a mood or something else?
LYAMAN:	No, it isn't.
MANHOLD:	She's as good as gold, so guileless.
IRA:	Guileless, I don't know about that.
MANHOLD:	Lyaman, are you as good as gold?
LYAMAN:	Gold is expensive.

MANHOLD: You see.

LYAMAN: I'm not a piece of gold.

IRA: Always this modesty of the East.
Basically it's nothing but arrogance.

MANHOLD: East or West, we've all gone broke by
now.

LAURENZ: Right you are!

EVI: I couldn't face my students like this, so
negatively.

IRA: Who is negative around here?

MANHOLD: Lyaman, are we negative?

LYAMAN: No, no, you aren't.

IRA: Alright, so now let's all dance, you,
Evi, Laurenz, Manhold too, and by all
means Lyaman. Dancing is a good
remedy for everything.

*The four of them move awkwardly and out of rhythm to the music
that has started anew. Manhold exaggerates his moves and
Laurenz does the same. Only Lyaman finds a graceful way of
moving to the music. Evi imitates Ira's movements which looks
ridiculous.*

ACT FIVE

They have stopped dancing and fling themselves onto the sofas.

MANHOLD: Lyaman, fetch some more wine, please.
Dancing makes you thirsty and all the
rest, too.

Lyaman jumps up and gets wine.

IRA: Dancing, at long last you do dance.
For me it's a proof that it's not too
late.

LAURENZ: Too late for what?

IRA: For life.

MANHOLD: Don't get that stagy, Ira. For you
dancing is like sex, for the rest of us
sex is just like sex.

EVI: Dancing is expression, sex is desire.

LAURENZ: Oh, really? None of us would ever
have thought of that.

Manhold drops a glass, everybody falls silent.

MANHOLD: Just like this glass here drops and
bursts, smashed into smithereens is

our livelihood. A minute ago I emptied this glass; a minute ago it was nicely filled to the brim. Everything can fall so fast: things we held in our hands so confidently and which we raised to our lips without a thought.

Ira gets up. She paces to and fro, bumps into Lyaman who had gone to fetch the wine. Lyaman stumbles, the wine slips from her hand. She kneels next to the puddle of wine.

IRA: Just get some new wine, Lyaman, will you. Don't you start cleaning up, I can't stand this now.

MANHOLD: Yes, do so, my child, simply get some new wine.

IRA: Why do you call her my child?

MANHOLD: Really, no need to weigh every word.

IRA: Isn't she quite your child of gold, this Lyaman?

LAURENZ: Child of gold, weighing gold, quite a play on words!

EVI: This is not a play on words.

Ira walks over to Laurenz. She stops in front of him and lets her dress drop down to her belly.

IRA: What do you think, Laurenz, are they still firm, my tits?

LAURENZ: Now, Ira!

IRA: Now, Ira! Now, Ira! These days even eighteen-year-olds go under the knife; as a forty year old woman I have all rights to ask whether you think my tits are firm.

LAURENZ: They, well, they are perfect.

IRA: Maybe they were once, so be honest.

EVI: Why do you ask Laurenz and not Manhold?

IRA: Because Manhold doesn't tell me the truth.

MANHOLD: Touch them, Laurenz, that's the only way to tell if they are really firm.

LAURENZ: I can't touch them just like that!

EVI: We have been to a club for couples once. Laurenz had been going on about that for weeks on end. We crossed half of Germany because of my school, you understand, as far away as possible, if this messing around was to be inevitable. So when we finally arrived, Laurenz behaved just like now, all cowered, like a heap of misery. I can't touch them just like that, that's Laurenz all over. At least I needn't be jealous, because Laurenz doesn't know the first thing about women. Women feel this straight away and lose all interest.

MANHOLD: And is he jealous?

LAURENZ: I'm not, have never been concerning Evi.

IRA: Touch them, Laurenz!

Laurenz touches Ira's breasts in a clumsy way, his hands tremble considerably. Manhold gives off a loud laugh. Lyaman stands, frozen in motion, in the middle of the room holding on to the carafe of wine she has just fetched. Evi coughs dryly.

MANHOLD: This is fun! What a lark! Finally the joint is jumping again. Laurenz, you ought to be grateful to me, my Cialis is giving you guts!

IRA: I can't decide what sickens me more, Manhold: when you are moody or when you are having fun.

MANHOLD *suddenly angry*: So alright, you go and pack your tits back, Ira, nobody here thinks this is funny.

Ira pulls up the dress to her shoulder. She walks over to the window which cannot be seen. Lyaman still stands in the middle of the room.

IRA: Alright, so the evening is to be played along your rules then, Manhold.

MANHOLD: That's crap; there are no rules, least of all mine.

IRA: There are; it's always been like this. All things have worked according to your rules. You've always said there were none; this has never been true. You have never asked me what I wanted.

MANHOLD: And what do you want, Ira? You see, I'm doing it now, I'm asking you, everybody can hear it: what do you want, Ira?

IRA: Not in this way, Manhold.

MANHOLD: Not this way, not that way, which way, then? I'm supposed to ask, so I ask, but then I'm told "not this way", does anybody get this? Evi, you as a woman, do you understand this?

EVI: Yes, I understand.

MANHOLD: Of course, women stick together, silly of me to ask. Laurenz, do you get this?

LAURENZ: I'd rather stay out of this.

MANHOLD: Oh really, want to stay out of this, do you? To write it all down later, or what?

LAURENZ: I'm discreet; I don't exploit things like this.

MANHOLD: Wow!

IRA: Nobody has ever asked me what I actually want. And today again nobody does. Nobody cares to know what I really want!

MANHOLD: Why not simply tell us, for heaven's sake!

IRA: Yes, I will do so!

Everybody looks at Ira, but she keeps quiet.

MANHOLD: I haven't heard a thing, have you?

EVI: Just leave her alone.

MANHOLD: Ira, maybe you don't know what you want, after all!

IRA: I want to dance.

Everyone groans, even Lyaman.

MANHOLD: Ira, this won't do. First you upset the
             apple cart and then...

IRA: Just look at yourselves, what a bunch
             of tight-ass, self-conscious, pathetic
             and ...

MANHOLD: And what?

IRA: ... completely unerotic people you are.

EVI: So that's how you perceive us?

LAURENZ: She could be right, though.

EVI: You've got no idea about eroticism,
             how do you think you can contribute?

LAURENZ: As much as you I definitely understand
             about it.

EVI: Sure, sure.

MANHOLD: You are just as tight-ass and self-
             conscious yourself, Ira.

IRA: I don't pop Cialis.

MANHOLD: Surprise, as a woman.

IRA: You all pop them and then go on
             complaining.

MANHOLD: We are not complaining, are we? Is
              anybody complaining here? Only you
              are complaining.

IRA: I want to be appreciated as a woman,
              is that asking too much? So we are
              broke; but at least I want to feel that
              I'm still a woman, a woman who is
              wanted.

All remain silent and perplexed. Lyaman serves the wine and carefully pours glass after glass. After that she sits down on a sofa. Laurenz runs a handkerchief over his entire head and down his neck. Evi opens two buttons of his shirt.

MANHOLD: Lyaman, let's have some music to lift
              our spirits, anything will do, music is
              best now.

Lyaman gets up, a short while later one can hear CRY BABY by Janis Joplin.

MANHOLD: We listened to stuff like this when we
              were young; strange, isn't it?

The music continues and nobody says a word anymore. Ira is standing at the window which is invisible. She seems to cry. When the music is over, everybody keeps silent for a long time.

MANHOLD: What power this music has. People
              those days were completely different.
              They made different music, they
              thought and felt differently.

LAURENZ: But they have gone down.

Manhold gets up and opens three buttons of his shirt.

MANHOLD: Gone down? And what do you think we are doing? We are also going down without ever having achieved something comparable to that music! Let me tell you something: once a month I have a heart attack and then I check into a hospital. They tell me that I'm as fit as a fiddle and that my heart attack is nothing but an illusion, a delusion with all indications of a real heart attack. All this happens because I'm going down and know so, whereas nobody else knows or even suspects so.

IRA: Manhold, don't overdo it so awfully.

MANHOLD: I'm not exaggerating, actually I'm even understating. My life is like this play we went to see the other day after having considered at length. Haven't been to the theatre for ages, let's support them, I said to Ira, one theatre after the other closing down these days. So we bought tickets and went. We were hardly seated and listened when the play was over, just an hour. We were out on the street after barely having entered the theatre. My life is like this, like this visit to the theatre. What a cheek to perform a play of just about one hour's length leaving no other trace except for the anger at the waste of money!

IRA: Well, at any rate, we've been to the theater again.

Manhold jumps up and shouts.

MANHOLD: No, not at any rate! What's that supposed to mean? At any rate we've been to the theatre again! That's a confession of failure! It's like wanting to have sex and looking forward to it. Then nothing happens and I tell myself, well, at any rate I've shaved my balls again!

IRA: Don't get so excited!

MANHOLD: I wish I were, as you say, excited. I wish I were!

IRA: So much for Cialis.

MANHOLD: You are never at a loss for a reply, are you?

IRA: Come on, show us your shaved balls!

MANHOLD: I haven't shaved them and even if I had, it wouldn't really mean a thing.

IRA: I bet Evi is unshaved.

EVI: But I'm not a man!

Laurenz laughs and sweats excessively.

IRA: Laurenz, you are perspiring so awfully,
             are you ill? There must be a reason for
             sweating so much.

EVI: It's the tension, that's all.

IRA: And you, Laurenz, do you shave so
             that you look like a little boy again?

Laurenz giggles and falls into a coughing attack.

IRA: I bet nobody here is shaved, because
             nobody here thinks of sex one might
             have, only of sex one would have liked
             to have but will never have.

MANHOLD: You would lose this bet.

IRA: Is that so?

MANHOLD: You honestly believe that anyone here
             would let you in on who of us is
             shaving?

IRA: Nobody is, I'll bet you!

EVI: It's quite possible to have sex without

depilating one's genitals.

LAURENZ: Yes, sure, you can.

MANHOLD: You can do lots of things; in the eighties everybody was hairy, men and women. But today nobody likes to get hair between the teeth; this needn't be any more nowadays.

LAURENZ: You shouldn't make a confession of faith of it, that's my opinion.

IRA: Bourgeois!

EVI: Why am I a bourgeois?

IRA: Bourgeois!

LAURENZ: Those hairs do have a function, you know....

IRA: Top bourgeois!

LAURENZ: If not, they wouldn't be where they are, those hairs.

IRA: You go for kids, I'll bet you do.

LAURENZ: For heaven's sake!

IRA: So I'm right! You had no idea what to do with my tits, I could tell.

MANHOLD: Lyaman, do you shave?

LYAMAN: Yes, I do, for hygienic reasons.

Manhold laughs out loud, he laughs and laughs. Then he runs across the room and kicks the sofas. The others, appalled, watch him. Ira pulls her dress up over her head. The lights die down.

ACT SIX

It is dark. The stage is without any light.

MANHOLD *shouts*: What's the matter with the lights? I can't believe it, they simply turn off power only because you are late settling the bills! How could it come to this! This is the scowl of the crash! Here they go, turning off my lifeblood, all my illumination!

IRA: Won't you have a look at the fuses…

MANHOLD: Lyaman, go and get me the torch, fast, please.

Lyaman seems to have bumped into the table. After a while the the light cone of a torch can be seen.

MANHOLD: Yes, the fuses, the fuses…

Lyman hands the light cone to Manhold. He can be heard cursing, while it stays dark for a bit longer. Then the light is on again. Ira stands around in the nude; Laurenz and Evi rub their eyes and stare at her.

MANHOLD: It was a short, how this fits. Don't we have enough shorts without the fuses blowing and sitting in the dark? As if we didn't sit in the dark anyway.

Ira moves as if posing for a photographer. She changes her position several times.

IRA: A naked woman can promote anything, I've done it for years on end; she can canvass anything except herself. On TV I've seen a group of naked parachuting girls promoting a detergent. One naked woman is not enough anymore nowadays, it's got to be an entire group, falling from the skies, of all things, only to draw attention to a detergent.
In those days a naked woman, pure and simple, could promote anything all by herself; but in those days and today she has never been permitted to canvass herself. If she does, they'll all consider her a slut straight away. That's where the loneliness stems from; with your bare skin you can promote anything except the important, the real thing that matters: you yourself. Models are coveted, but lonely, nobody can imagine just how lonely.

MANHOLD: What a performance, Ira!

IRA: Lyaman, get me a wool blanket, will you? I'm cold.

EVI: What a figure you've still got!

IRA: As you say, it's still…

LAURENZ: You've stayed young!

*Ira utters a brief and agonized laugh. Lyaman hurries along with
a woolen blanket. Ira takes it, but lets it drop. Lyaman bends
down, picks up the blanket and passes it to Ira who drops it
again. Lyaman bends down and when bending upwards again is
embraced fiercely by Ira.*

IRA: That takes you by surprise, doesn't it?
                  We could be girlfriends, you and me; I
                  could be twenty just like you. We
                  could both be au-pairs, but in a rich
                  house, not with bankrupts like
                  Manhold. We might be carrying on in
                  secret and dream of a future that
                  couldn't be brighter. Kiss me, Lyaman
                  or are you disgusted at me?

*Lyaman stands around, frozen, while Ira, in despair, is touching
her all over.*

MANHOLD: Come on, Lyman, give her a kiss, and
                  let's put an end to this misery.

LAURENZ: Yes, go and kiss her, this turns me on.

EVI: This is close to abuse.

MANHOLD: She's already twenty, an adult, and
                  totally grown up.

EVI: But she's a dependant.

LAURENZ: So what?

EVI: I beg your pardon?

LAURENZ: What the hell!

EVI: You are horrid; I don't know you
               anymore.

LAURENZ: Because you've never known me
               anyway.

Lyaman shyly pecks Ira's cheek. Ira moves a bit away from her.

IRA: A kiss of pity! I deserve better than
               that. I should have known what you
               get if you open up to a country
               bumpkin! No passion, only
               astonishment, no lust, only rejection
               and scorn.

MANHOLD: What do you expect, Ira? That she
               seizes an opportunity she doesn't even
               want?

IRA *screaming*: Yes, that's what I expect! A tiny bit of
               respect, a little passion and at least
               being a bit surprised, that's what I
               expect!

Lyaman awakens from her frozen state and kisses Ira lovingly.

IRA: Too late, Lyaman, this wasn't on impulse, you did this just to please us all, all except me. Had you meant me, you would have kissed me like this from the start. Come on, pass me that blanket, you are as cold as ice.

Ira wraps up in the blanket and sinks into the sofa. Lyaman, embarrassed, sits down next to her. Manhold picks up the carafe, fills up his glass, gulps it down and a second one straight away. Laurenz sits with his eyes closed.

MANHOLD: Laurenz, what's the matter with you?

LAURENZ: I feel like I was drained, sort of weak. I think I've got a spell of dizziness.

EVI: Weak you are in any case; you don't need a dizzy spell for that.

MANHOLD: We are all weak, even in our biggest strength.

Ira screams, shakes her hair and screams.

IRA: I can't stand this any longer! We'll go to the social welfare office, Manhold and me; Manhold will do lots of explaining and commenting, but nobody is going to listen to a loser, no matter how much he raked in in the past.
And I, the model, the former model,

will meet looks fraught with hostility. They will leave through my curriculum vitae like you do with yesterday's newspaper, even worse, they will look at me like someone who hasn't deserved better.

MANHOLD: What's this talk about the social welfare office?

IRA: That's what all this is heading for! Whatever else?

MANHOLD: A handful of peanuts   they'll offer you there...

IRA: Manhold, we are broke!

MANHOLD: It's all a matter of perspective; I know people who are much worse off.

IRA: Very soon you won't be able to pay Lyaman's pocket money any more, the same for the bread you eat!

MANHOLD: You are exaggerating, a customer might come along tomorrow and then we pick up pace again.

IRA: No customer will come to you any longer.

MANHOLD: How come? No customer coming

	along for me any more?
IRA:	Yes, yes, don't you realize this, it's the truth, after all!
MANHOLD:	No more customers! How absurd is this! As if everything would just come to an end! People will always advertise!
IRA:	But today twenty-year-olds are doing this. They wouldn't even look at you or greet you. They wouldn't want any dealings with you at all.
MANHOLD:	Greenhorns!
IRA:	You call them greenhorns, I say they are professionals and professionals are what everybody is calling them.
MANHOLD:	Raw recruits!
IRA:	I can't possibly walk the streets to feed us both!
MANHOLD:	No, you can't.
IRA:	Why can't I?
MANHOLD:	Because you are too old, as simple as that.
IRA:	Too old?

MANHOLD:	Too old, that's the way life goes.
IRA:	And if I were young?
MANHOLD:	I you were, well, if you were…
IRA:	I hate you.
MANHOLD:	No, you hate being too old.
EVI:	Young or old, this idea is definitely out of question from an ethical point of view, isn't it?
LAURENZ:	This kind of thing as a book, a total no-go. Everybody would believe the entire story a fabrication.
EVI:	This is too much, this is an abyss!
MANHOLD:	You look after your abyss; we've got ours here, no matter being a teacher.
EVI:	I don't have any abyss.
MANHOLD:	Your abyss is the complete mediocrity of it all!
LAURENZ:	You've got a point there…
EVI:	I don't have to put up with this, I'm leaving!

Evi stays seated. Lyaman puts her arm consolingly around Ira.

IRA:	Now you are coming to much, now when it's too late.
LYAMAN:	I don't understand all of this. Why is everybody so unhappy?
IRA:	Guess why?
LYAMAN:	Women who are as beautiful as you are rare back home and they are highly revered. They are not unhappy, the others are, those who cannot compare to them are distressed.
IRA:	Do you think I'm beautiful?
LYAMAN:	Yes, I do!
IRA:	And why don't I turn you on?
LYAMAN:	Because you are a woman and me, too.
IRA:	So what?
LYAMAN:	It doesn't match.
IRA:	But it can match if one wants it to.
MANHOLD:	Now what's this, what's going on here?
IRA:	You don't get it anyway.
LYAMAN:	Yes, it can, if one wants it to.

IRA:	And you don't want to, right?
LYAMAN:	I've got to think about it…
LAURENZ:	It's tearing me apart…
MANHOLD:	Why on earth?
LAURENZ:	All this pain!
MANHOLD:	I knew your books are pompous.
LAURENZ:	What's that? Why?
MANHOLD:	You are the typical guest who takes it all in, getting a kick out of all, and then, back at home, you pass judgment in your self-righteous way, condemning all and everyone and, like in your case, topping it all by writing it down.
LAURENZ:	So you think that ill of me?
MANHOLD:	I don't think ill of you, I'm just being realistic.
EVI:	I should have left long ago, all this is simply agonizing.
MANHOLD:	Go on, go home, Evi. Maybe that will get Laurenz going.

EVI: This is so ridiculous!

*Ira and Lyaman kiss each other passionately. The others watch
them, completely exhausted. Manhold gets up, goes over to the
stereo and presses a button. The sound of* Heaven Stood Still
*by Willy de Ville can be heard. Manhold takes off his shirt and
mops the sweat off his forehead and from his armpits.*

MANHOLD: Willy de Ville is dead. It's only a
question of time when we'll be gone, too.

EVI: Where is the connection, please?

MANHOLD: I knew you would ask something like
                this.

EVI: It doesn't hurt to ask, surely.

Manhold shouts.

MANHOLD: You dumb fool! You abominable soul!
                You eternal teacher!
                You cold nothing!

Everyone pauses. Lyaman holds Ira's hand.

LAURENZ: He's not completely wrong.

EVI: One is a guest here and gets insulted.

*Ira throws off the woolen blanket and sits on the sofa in the nude.
Manhold gulps down the wine.*

ACT SEVEN

Manhold jumps up, the others stay seated. Laurenz pulls at the blanket. Lyaman is still holding Ira's hand. Evi sips at the wine.

MANHOLD: If you only knew when things are starting to go wrong, but don't notice. You are so cocksure, you don't look closely any longer and then there you are, looking down an abyss, even though you've only been for a short stroll.

Failure comes along without you noticing it. It comes along like some soft spring air delivering death to you, though winter should have brought death along. However, spring does the job. It's not by chance that most people kill themselves in spring and not in autumn.

Everything has gone wrong, but that bothers me less than not having noticed it at all.

LAURENZ: Alright, so we are broke, but we aren't dead, are we?

MANHOLD: Isn't a wash-out the same as death?

LAURENZ: Death is in Port-au-Prince.

MANHOLD: Yes, in Port-au-Prince, that's where

death is.

EVI: You two ought to be ashamed of yourselves comparing your sniveling complaints to a real tragedy.

MANHOLD: We could go by plane down there, the five of us and help rebuilding things. I do mean it. There is nothing to do for us here, no need for people like us.

LAURENZ: Even there we'd only be in the way.

MANHOLD: I could do documentaries, photographic ones, I mean.

IRA: The only things you've ever taken pictures of were girly-girls.

MANHOLD: Time to change that.

LAURENZ: Take it from me, we'd only mess up things.

MANHOLD: Helping, that would be a new attitude to life!

LAURENZ: How on earth would we be of any help!

MANHOLD: Dropping everything and try something new, going down to Haiti!

EVI: Don't run roughshod with your talks!

IRA: I'm sure they are just waiting for you
             to come along!

MANHOLD: I've never done any good in my life.
             All I've ever done was animating
             people to consume more crap. I've
             never helped anyone, I've come to
             realize that only now!

IRA: Help me; that would be something for
             a start.

MANHOLD: You can back yourself; am I your
             nurse? Besides, you've got Lyaman
             now. Just look at the two of you,
             sitting there, holding hands, simply
             ridiculous!

LAURENZ: To tell the truth, we aren't needed
             anywhere. Maybe Evi, in school, that's
             about it. But teachers are replaceable,
             too, just like anyone going to work is
             replaceable. Just like any job can be
             replaced at random by any other.

MANHOLD: All l meet these days are frostiness and
             aloofness. Appointments are not kept
             any more, shootings are ignored and
             models don't show up. Customers
             request offers without ever so much as
             an answer. I get threatened by debt
             collectors, I get threatened all the time
             by everyone, by people I don't even

know whom I'm supposed to owe
something. Frostiness, rejection and
silence, that's all. Horrible silence, as if
the phone was out of order, as if I
were cut off the internet, as if I were
not among the living any longer.
You get up in the morning, but you
don't know why; maybe out of habit,
maybe because even the longest night
will end eventually. But then my day
starts like a night, because my days are
like nights, as silent and dark as they
are.

IRA: Manhold, this is unbearable.

MANHOLD: That's it, it's simply unbearable.

IRA: You are the one who is unbearable.

MANHOLD: Oh, really, so it's me now. And if I
            can't stand you anymore you are hurt
            or what?

IRA: You won't change a thing by all your
            talks, just call it quits.

MANHOLD: So what am I supposed to do?
            Nobody can give me advice; nobody
            can help me, because nobody wants to
            help me. I'm at a loss for what to do.
            I'll die in the best of health, yes,
            exactly, that's it! You die and nobody

notices. That's the way we all live, with this sort of backdrop.

People who argue to the contrary are on the wrong track. People who won't accept this are fooling themselves, just as I've been fooling myself for years regarding my own person and my place in society. You've got to see things like I'm doing now.

My family was always so good to me, everybody cheery and in high spirits all the time. Money was never an issue, large home, gigantic garden, holiday home, three cars and life insurances. I was pampered, I was loved; they took care of me, they doted on me, I was the sunshine of the entire family.

And now all my family is dead, I am the last member of my entire family. All the money has been squandered. There is no one anymore to whom I am sunshine and hope; nobody there to take me by the hand when I'm afraid of the world.

This is my end; this is what my end looks like. It's as if there had never been a past, as if I were trapped in eternal present time.

IRA: It's always your family you come up with!

MANHOLD: It's only now that I realize just how

infinite their love for me was!

IRA: You complained about them all the time!

MANHOLD: Never!

IRA: Without end, you pulled them to pieces!

MANHOLD: If I did so, if I did at all, I called them names out of love.

EVI: If that's how you remember it, then I think you really do need therapy!

MANHOLD: Me?

EVI: I know a good psychologist who...

MANHOLD: You talk a bit about your sorrows and off you go telling me about a psychologist! What would I tell that guy? Digital photography is breaking my neck, I'd say, it's driving me into bankruptcy, it's my undoing, leading customers all of a sudden to take pictures themselves! What, do you think, he could reply to that? I've got a digital camera myself, he'd say.

EVI: I just thought it might be helpful perhaps.

MANHOLD: That's not helpful, what's crossing your mind about me and my situation is beside the point and neither here nor there.

IRA: So now it's turned into only your situation?

MANHOLD: Yes, it's mine!

IRA: And what about me?

MANHOLD: It's only you I'm thinking of when I worry about things!

IRA: All you care about is yourself!

MANHOLD: Believe whatever you like, but I do care about both of us; I've always done that.

EVI: I always consider Laurenz, too when I think of myself; I care about the two of us, I do, though I don't know why I'm doing that, considering how self-indulgent Laurenz is these days.

LAURENZ: I'm not self-indulgent, every day I sit there writing, it's agony, nobody can imagine what it's like to finally make it to page one hundred, it's a marathon!

EVI: Books nobody reads.

LAURENZ: So what! The main thing is that they've been written, these books!

MANHOLD: Can't you forget your books for once tonight? Are the Cialis really without any effect on you? Can this be true?

LAURENZ: Cialis, Cialis, of course I had to take them, only I can be that stupid!

MANHOLD: Nothing excites you any more; actually you are an old man, no longer good for anything.

LAURENZ: You can't offend me, I know who I am and I know who I used to be.

MANHOLD: Yes, sure, a managing director. High and mighty Managing Director Laurenz! Complete with secretary and driver and all the trimmings! You can write your memoirs now!

LAURENZ: Nobody can hurt me, least of all you.

MANHOLD: Why least of all me? Because I'm a loser? Tell me straight to my face if you think so!

LAURENZ: Loser!

MANHOLD: Respect! Hats off! Wouldn't have thought you have the guts! So, not all

	is lost speaking of you. Ira, go and check out his crotch, I bet you'll only hold limp fry there in your hand without the slightest twitch!
IRA:	Why don't you go and check out yourself!
MANHOLD:	God forbid!
LAURENZ:	I'm not impotent, in case you are insinuating that.
EVI:	We've got regular…
MANHOLD:	Wow, regular, so what is it you've got regularly? Sunday sermon, country broadcast?
EVI:	We've got a fulfilling sex life.

Manhold shrieks and laughs, running across the living room, kicking the back of the sofa a couple of times on which Laurenz and Evi are squatting. He takes off his trousers and, clad in shorts with a flower pattern, darts around the two sofas.

MANHOLD: I'm sorry, I'm so sorry!

He laughs, he can hardly stop laughing.

MANHOLD: Boy, haven't I been real naughty again, same as ever, bad Manhold, just can't keep his trap shut. To compensate for

that I've got the most awful underwear
you can imagine. I'm showing it only
to get into a better mood.

IRA: Nobody here has got a fulfilling sex
life, Evi.

EVI: But we do.

IRA: You needn't say that, this will lead to
nothing. Nobody believes it, even you
don't, let alone Laurenz. I mean, at our
age, there isn't any more to say such a
thing.

EVI: Alright, alright, so there is nothing
doing, dead as a doornail, does that
sound better?

IRA: Much better!

MANHOLD: Very much better!

LAURENZ: Dead as a doornail!

MANHOLD: Dead as a doornail!

IRA: Dead as a doornail! Sounds good! How
true this is! How plain and clear-cut!
It's great to say that sort of thing, just
like that!

EVI: Dead as a doornail, what a relief not to

have to beat about the bush anymore!

MANHOLD: That's it! Exactly! You've got to stick by it!

IRA: And why do you pop Cialis, if you stick by it?

MANHOLD: No need to get fussy, I also pop aspirins without having a headache, simply because I like popping aspirins; I pop Cialis simply because…

LAURENZ: Because of what?

MANHOLD: No idea.

EVI: That's not true. You pop them because you plan to do something.

MANHOLD: But don't you see that I'm not doing anything; so I can't very well plan to do something.

EVI: And why do you undress?

MANHOLD: Only because I'm too warm!

EVI: If everybody stripped just because they feel warm!

LAURENZ: Why not let him strip, it doesn't bother me. Ira is in the nude, too and it doesn't bother me either.

IRA: How very gracious of you, Laurenz;
you do have a knack of paying
compliments to a woman.

MANHOLD: I guess we agree on this; after all, we
do get along, we get on well, all of us;
I'd say we get on like a house on fire.
We are all grown-ups, looking back on
many years and not all of them have
been bad, on the contrary.
This crisis is something that will go by,
it's a temporary thing, nothing final,
not for good. It's not the end we are
so terrified of. Our situation is
provisional, momentary. It's only our
fear, that's all and a bit of teasing won't
do any harm to our friendship, will it?

IRA: So calm, Manhold? Sure you didn't
pop Valium by mistake instead of
Cialis?

MANHOLD: Valium?

LAURENZ: Valium?

IRA: Sure, the two of you act as if you had
popped Valium. Like they had taken
Valium, right, Lyaman?

LYAMAN: I'm not sure.

IRA: You needn't.

MANHOLD: You drive for settlement and harmony
                and straight away they suspect you of
                having taken sleeping pills. What now?
                What am I supposed to do? Dance
                with Laurenz? Tear the clothes off
                Evi?

EVI: For God's sake…

MANHOLD: I popped Cialis, not Valium, I took
                Cialis, like Laurenz did and my cock
                will be up and alive whenever I feel
                like it.

Lyaman giggles.

MANHOLD: Wow, you figured that out real fast,
                Lyaman.

LYAMAN: Sorry.

MANHOLD: No need to apologize for that.

IRA: No, not for that.

*Manhold takes off his draws and stands in front of Ira and
                Lyaman.*

MANHOLD: This is maddening! This turns you
                crazy. All of this is driving me round
                the bend this very night!

IRA: There isn't a thing up and alive!

MANHOLD: How could there be when the fear for
                your very survival takes your breath
                away, all the yearning and guts you've
                got.

EVI: As if nobody here had ever seen a man
                in the nude!

LAURENZ: Respect, Manhold; I wouldn't go this
                far!

LYAMAN: Well, I really don't know…

IRA: You've got to cope with this, Lyaman;
                you are a grown-up woman, after all.

MANHOLD: It's driving me nuts, no matter what
                you do, people don't make you out,
                neither in refusing nor in allowing
                something. I'd say lust is being
                overrated, the desire for close
                company is underrated, I'm sure you'd
                agree on that.

IRA: Manhold, do just sit down here, next
                to Lyaman and me, won't you?

MANHOLD: And where is the snag?

IRA: Only you can think of something like
                that!

MANHLD: There's got to be a snag…

LYMAN: Please sit down next to us, it's such an
             ugly evening.

*Manhold sits down next to Ira and Lyaman. Lyaman caresses
Manhold's arms, Ira caresses Lyman. Laurenz' face is twitching,
Evi is quivering all over.*

MANHOLD: Okay like this?

IRA: Yes, this is just fine.

LYMAN: Now the evening is alright.

LAURENZ: I think I'm in the wrong movie.

EVI: Dead as a doornail!

MANHOLD: Right, dead as a doornail!

IRA: Dead pants!

LYAMAN: Pants can't be dead if you are not
             wearing the breeches.

MANHOLD: How smart she is! Besides, pants are
             always dead, whether you've got them
             on or off.

IRA: Lyaman, you are real smart!

MANHOLD: So smart, can't compare to any other
             girl!

EVI: Is this smart or just shrewd?

LAURENZ: Speaking of me, I guess I did pop
            Valium.

ACT EIGHT

Ira and Lyaman are seated, holding hands, as before. Ira whispers something into Lyaman's ear. Lyman shakes her head and exits.

MANHOLD: What did you tell her?

IRA: What I told her?

MANHOLD: Yes, what did you say to her?

IRA: That she should get undressed.

MANHOLD: That so?

IRA: For solidarity's sake…

MANHOLD: Wrong idea of solidarity…

IRA: There is no such thing as misunderstanding of solidarity.

MANHOLD: For Lyaman it's nothing but a trip into absurdity, a side trip into the decadence of the West which is, after all, known for its depravity in the Eastern world.

IRA: Lyaman ought to prove herself.

MANHOLD: As what?

IRA: As au-pair…

MANHOLD: That's cynical, Ira. It's hard on her to have come to people like us.

IRA: You think so?

MANHOLD: Yes, I do!

IRA: There are au-pairs who happen to get into conceited families. Their lot is not easier than Lyaman's who came across us; maybe we are a bit testing, but we are definitely not snobbish. We are possibly a bit peculiar, but we are genuine.

MANHOLD: But there are also au-pairs who get a totally regular family…

IRA: Aren't we regular? We've got the little one and …

MANHOLD: And?

IRA: Yes, and …

MANHOLD: We are not regular, we are in a predicament, in a quagmire, we are not a family at all and if we are one, then we are a family which is breaking down.

IRA: Yes, yes, yes.

MANHOLD: We are taking things too far with Lyaman, that is, you are going too far. You are distressing her. She doesn't grasp this. She doesn't understand us.

IRA: I don't get her either; maybe she understands much more than we think.

MANHOLD: Yes, could be.

LAURENZ: A silly little girl!

EVI: What a silly little girl!

IRA: So what! Maybe that's just so!

MANHOLD: Maybe that's just so!

IRA: Exactly!

MANHOLD: Exactly!

Lyaman returns wrapped up in a woolen blanket.

IRA: Very good!

MANHOD: Well done!

LAURENZ: Very good!

EVI: Oh well, as you please.

Lyaman: Her I am, back again.

IRA: Drop it, that wool blanket!

LYAMAN: But I'd be nude then!

IRA: Right, you'd be nude then!

MANHOLD: That would be nice!

LAURENZ: Naked!

EVI: All of them here want to see you in the nude!

IRA: Do it for me, drop it!

LYAMAN: Oh, I really don't know!

IRA: It doesn't make a difference now anymore!

LYAMAN: I'll simply drop it?

IRA: Precisely!

MANHOLD: Precisely!

EVI: I won't comment on this any more.

Lyaman drops the woolen blanket.

IRA: How beautiful you are!

MANHOLD: Yes, you are!

IRA: How innocent!

MANHOLD: If I had known how beautiful your
            body is!

IRA: Shaved so expertly!

MANHOLD: For hygienic reasons, she told us,
            didn't she?

IRA: So clean-shaven!

MANHOLD: Clean-shaven!

LAURENZ: Smooth like a child!

EVI: She just acts like she were the country
            innocent, actually she is quite crafty.

MANHOLD: Completely shaven!

IRA: There!

MANHOLD: So you do comply with what Ira has
            been asking, coming to us like this.

LYAMAN: I adapt to the customs of the people!

MANHOLD: Nothing wrong with that.

IRA: Not wrong at all!

MANHOLD: Definitely not wrong!

LYAMAN: That's why I came along with the blanket, that's why I even dropped it.

MANHOLD: Yes, I get it.

IRA: Lyaman, I've underrated you!

EVI: She's hot stuff and only posing the don't-touch-me-miss, just like she's been waiting all along to play to the gallery like this.

LAURENZ: Hot stuff, how dare you suggest something like that! What a lot of contempt you've got.

IRA: Lyaman, don't listen; you've done a good job, I'm proud of you. Come on, sit down next to me again, won't you?

EVI: What sort of game is this supposed to be, Ira?

IRA: This is no game.

EVI: Manhold, you tell me then.

MANHOLD: We are relaxing, that's all. Despite all the trouble one happens to have, a serious attempt to relax shouldn't be left untried.

EVI:	You call that relaxing? To sit there in the nude on the sofa, along with your au-pair, while you are having guests?
MANHOLD:	Yes, among other things.
EVI:	This is sick!
LAURENZ:	I don't think so. I think it's uncommon, basically not really objectionable.
EVI:	Write about it, for all I care, but don't talk such drivel.
MANHOLD:	The way we are sitting here I can feel tension losing its hold on me.
IRA:	I feel the same. How about you, Lyaman, how does it make you feel?
LYAMAN:	When in Rome, do as the Romans do, that's what they told us when we were placed, when they entered us in their register.
IRA:	But didn't they also warn you?
LYAMAN:	They did, they did.
IRA:	Of people like us?
LYAMAN:	No, no, you are good; Manhold is a

good man and you, you are so
beautiful, you are an exceptional
woman. But so sad, always sad.
Manhold and you, both so sad, I can
feel it, I can see it. It's not as if I didn't
notice things, I've got a keen sense.

MANHOLD: She understands us! It takes a girl from
Azerbaijan to be understood!

LYAMAN: If you are afraid of poverty, you don't
realize that you are still rich, because
the poverty I've known looks quite
different.

IRA: Maybe so.

LYAMAN: Your fear is so enormous because
there is nobody, nobody around you.
At my place things are different, even
the poor are not alone. They are poor,
but not lonely. Here it seems as if
poverty and loneliness were one single
word. Back home...

MANHOLD: Yes, what's it like back at your home?

LYAMAN: Completely different.

MANHOLD: I guess so.

IRA: Lyaman, have you got a boyfriend?

LYAMAN: No, I haven't.

IRA: A girlfriend?

LYMAN: Yes, of course I have.

IRA: And what would she think, seeing you
             sitting with us like this?

LYAMAN: She'd think that I've got bad luck.

MANHOLD: There you are, bad luck, when all's said
             and done Lyaman is just unlucky with
             us.

LYAMAN: But my girlfriend wouldn't be able to
             grasp that I'm fortunate, not miserable.
             To grasp this she would have to be
             me.

EVI: What kind of talks!

LAURENZ: Leave her alone, I want to listen,
             sometimes you can learn something
             from that, for yourself, too and your
             own situation.

EVI: What sort of thing would you learn
             from this, witnessing such an utterly
             absurd show?

LAURENZ: I think it's heart-rending what
             Lyaman is telling us.

MANHOLD: Yes, it is, Laurenz, you are absolutely right, it's truly heart-rending and I'm saying this without any mockery.

IRA: You've been living with us for weeks now, Lyaman, but I've never been quite aware of you, really.

MANHOLD: For me you you've been just a nanny and I who's had so many women and who's photographed so many models, I have never seen the woman in you at all.

EVI: Another sexual object!

MANHOLD: No, that's exactly not the point.

EVI: You are fooling yourself, there is no stopping anymore! You got the green light!

MANHOLD: This is not so.

IRA: And if it were so!

EVI: Do you approve?

IRA: Yes, I do approve.

MANHOLD: Ira, don't let yourself be provoked.

IRA: In this situation human nearness is the

most important thing for me, the one and only, the true deliverance. All this phony morality, I don't give a hoot, it's never been a help, not in small disasters, let alone in big ones.

MANHOLD: Thanks to Lyaman you are getting alive again, Ira.

IRA: Yes.

MANHOLD: You and me, both getting alive and it won't be to Lyaman's disadvantage, either.

LYAMAN: I won't tell anybody.

IRA: What is it you won't tell?

LYAMAN: That I'm sitting here with you, in the nude.

IRA: Because you are ashamed?

LYAMAN: No, it's because I'm not ashamed that I won't tell anybody. Nobody would understand me, they would all despise me, despise you and damn you. Everybody would think I was the victim and you the offenders, but you are no offenders and I am not a victim. I learn a lot, I see a lot. Since I've come here I've learnt a lot. I discover

	things which are too complicated to tell about.
IRA:	I'd really love to have a daughter like you.
MANHOLD:	Yes, such a daughter, that would be happiness!
EVI:	That would be incest!
LAURENZ:	But they aren't doing a thing, just sitting there together on the sofa.
EVI:	For me, this is getting awfully close to abuse! Anyway, it's completely preposterous, the very idea of Lyaman being your daughter.
IRA:	Daughter and girlfriend, all in one.
MANHOLD:	Daughter, girlfriend, playmate, all in one.
EVI:	See, I told you so! Nothing will hold you back now!
MANHOLD:	It's just daydreaming, that's all.
EVI:	Dreaming, that's all you do. That's why your life is all in shambles.
MANHOLD:	So, I won't be moved up now, is that

	it? Must I repeat class now?
EVI:	No need to comment this.
LAURENZ:	Lyaman is teaching us!
MANHOLD:	Yes, she is showing us that we have no idea of life.
IRA:	Lyaman, now you can see me the way I am, I've completely underrated you!
LYAMAN:	You need peace. You have no friends.
EVI:	And what are we?

Everyone keeps quiet. Ira is caressing Lyman, Lyaman is caressing Manhold. Laurenz is curling up on the sofa like a baby. Evi gets up.

EVI:	I'm calling a taxi now.
LAURENZ:	Alright, do so.
EVI:	I will.
LAURENZ:	Get going, will you?
EVI:	But in half an hour I'll really call a taxi.

Ira kisses Lyaman passionately.

ACT NINE

Ira is stroking Lyaman's hair. Evi averts her eyes, Laurenz looks very closely, Manhold is looking up at the ceiling.

MANHOLD: Lyaman, be so kind and get us some more supplies, the wine is gone again.

Lyaman gets up and goes in the nude to the kitchen which is not visible. Manhold's eyes are following her.

MANHOLD: That's the way we will do things from now on.

IRA: Right, it's going to be like this always.

MANHOLD: To think that it's taken us this long to get the idea! That we've not been aware of Lyaman, she is so open now. She ought to stay with us for ever; that will give us strength and confidence.

IRA: At long last I've got a girlfriend.

MANHOLD: And a daughter.

EVI: Here we go again! Is there no end to this?

MANHOLD: It's the very young people who can really open your eyes, only the very young and therefore fresh and better

	people can do this. They make us focus again on the important matters.
IRA:	Yes, she should stay with us for ever.
MANHOLD:	I'm all for it.
IRA:	Let's tell her straight away that this is possible.
MANHOLD:	That's going to be a big surprise!
IRA:	I'm so happy for her!
MANHOLD:	Let's tell her as soon as she comes back with the wine.
LAURENZ:	You'd better think about it twice, too much closeness can be a bother. I'm thinking about the two of you and your privacy.
MANHOLD:	Come off it! Too much closeness doesn't bother us. Actually we are looking for a closeness which is different from the standard one.
IRA:	We are looking for something like this, being honestly close, the truly human factor, the great friendship, the unconditional amour, loving. Loving which is more than mere lust, that's what we've been looking for. It's just

that we have never known.

Lyaman enters the living room, holding a carafe in her hand. She stops and regards Ira and Manhold.

MANHOLD: Ah, there you are, back again. There is something we'd like to discuss with you, Ira and me.

LYAMAN: I was also going to say something.

MANHOLD: That so? Great! So you start, our issue can wait a bit longer. But don't keep standing there, come on over to us and bring along the wine.

Lyaman stays put, she does not move. Everyone is looking at her, Manhold and Ira look increasingly blank.

LYAMAN: I like accommodating, I always accommodate, but I want to leave this house, as early as tomorrow. I have learnt a lot here, but it's too complicated for me, I…

MANHOLD: Lyaman, we are all in the same boat and now you want to swim away suddenly? All by yourself?

IRA: But we are friends, we've only now kissed each other …

LYAMAN: We'll always stay friends…

IRA: How could we when you are gone?

LYAMAN: I can't stay her, I would lose myself.
Even now I'm no longer my true self. I
walk around here like a whore.

MANHOLD: Not at all, you aren't doing that at all.
A whore is something totally different,
the exact opposite of all the things you
are.

LYAMAN: Everybody back home would see me
that way.

MANHOLD: The people back home don't always
know better.

LYAMAN: Those at home know me.

IRA: And us, we've come to know you, too.

LYAMAN: As naked girl who brings along the
wine and who you kiss. I know how
this would go on. It would never stop
at kissing, never at all the friendliness
that's still there.

MANHOLD: I promise you…

LYAMAN: My mind is made up…

IRA: Ira, dear, let's talk about it
reasonably…

LYAMAN: I don't want to stay.

MANHOLD *jumps up and yells*: You rascal, you've
                    fooled us all! You've tricked yourself
                    into our trust, just to let us down, this
                    is the last straw!

LYAMAN: No, but…

IRA: Nice kind of friendship, so this is what
                    you call friendship! Now you are the
                    street girl you allegedly didn't want to
                    be, all naked, but the very picture of
                    no emotional commitment at all! And
                    all this folksy stuff, you pull that out of
                    your hat whenever things get a bit
                    uncomfortable for you, when you have
                    to prove yourself, when you are
                    supposed to represent something!

LYAMAN: But I don't want to hurt anybody…

MANHOLD: You small town slut, what fools you've
                    made of us! You must have had the
                    time of your life, you and your
                    Cossacks over there…

LYAMAN: At our place…

MANHOLD: Don't interrupt me; I don't give a
                    damn for any Cossacks. If there is a
                    free fighter, it's me and not some
                    shifty men who send their daughters to

walk the street as au-pair.

LAURENZ: Manhold, you are taking this too far!

EVI: Horrible! But I've known all along, a little stupid thing, sly and mean…

LYAMAN: But I've only wanted to …

IRA: Alright then, if you can't bear our company, if you find us so revolting, then I guess you'll have to leave.

MANHOLD: Nothing but revolting and self-centered things comes from the young ones, that and undiluted egotism! You have no idea of humaneness. You are at home in barbarity and that's where you are comfortable! To seduce a woman like Iris in such a way only to abandon her immediately afterwards, that is cruel. I won't even go into my case here! Shame on you, Lyaman!

Lyaman starts crying; she lets the carafe slip with a boom; she runs from the room, sobbing. The other four look down at the floor. For a long while no one dares to say a thing. Then:

LAURENZ: What did I tell you!

EVI: Laurenz, please, will you spare us…

LAURENZ: So what's the moral of the story then?

MANHOLD *in a subdued voice*: There is none. There is
no moral to the story, just as there is
no straightforwardness in the chaos of
life, no direction, no logic, no justice,
no gratitude, no reason and no
justification. The moral of the story?
Sure, that'd be something, if there was
one!

EVI: Manhold, you should be glad that she's
leaving, she only upsets you two.

MANHOLD: I'm not glad, I'm…

LAURENZ: A nice dream bubble has burst, not
more, not less.

MANHOLD: What would you know of my dreams!

IRA: I guess you are satisfied now, seeing us
fooled like that…

EVI: Didn't you fool yourselves?

LAURENZ: No, you can't put it that way…

IRA: Well, maybe, perhaps we did, but so
what? There aren't any losers tonight,
because everything has been lost
anyway for a long time.

MANHOLD: Lyaman, that silly girl, showing off
with her youth, her bloom, just you

wait and see, there won't be much left
in a couple of years. Then she will
come, knocking on our door, but our
door will stay shut.

IRA: I want her out of my sight, putting her
tongue down my throat and then
pulling off that kind of show!

MANHOLD: Stripping in front of us while her bags
are packed, that's downright
outrageous!

EVI: Indeed!

LAURENZ: You can't have faith in anything; reality
tops anything you can imagine!

MANHOLD: Such a slut doesn't impress me, it
needs a bit more than that! And the
women kept coming and going at my
place, I can assure you. I know the
ropes, I noticed right away that there is
something odd about Lyaman.

IRA: You could see that at once, we just
didn't say anything, for discretion's
sake.

*Evi gets up, Laurenz puts his shoes on again. Ira is cold and
wraps the wool blanket around her. Manhold hurriedly puts on
trousers and shirt.*

EVI:	I'm calling a taxi now.
LAURENZ:	Don't take it too hard, you can't help setbacks.
MANHOLD:	Do you take me for a chap who could take such a trifle seriously?
IRA:	We'll look for another au-pair, they are ten a penny. Pity though, the little one liked Lyaman a lot, but he'll like the next girl just as much.
LAURENZ:	Talking of jobs, things will look up, you bet on that!
MANHOLD:	I used to canvass that I can take shots of everything as long as the price is alright. I'm a professional, when people get knocked out I'm the one who gets up again. You see them all stretched out on the ground, but I'm up in no time at all!
LAURENZ:	The idea of a disaster is to emerge stronger than before. It will make you tougher than ever.
MANHOLD:	That's the way I see it, too.
IRA:	We've overcome quite different sorts of disasters!

EVI: When you are down and out, suddenly
              a light will shine…

LAURENZ: That's why I'm writing, because I don't
              give up; you shouldn't either, because
              hope dies last.

EVI: We should meet again.

IRA: Sure, we should definitely do it again.

MANHOLD: As soon as possible!

LAURENZ: I'm all for it!

EVI: Good night!

LAURENZ: A fascinating night, it's been a real
              treat!

IRA: Good night, my dears, get home safely!

MANHOLD: Keep a stiff upper lip, let's phone
              again!

The four of them kiss, after that Evi and Laurenz leave.

ACT TEN

Manhold hears Lyaman crying in the kitchen. She does not stop crying; she seems to be inconsolable.

MANHOLD: Lyaman!

IRA: Ah, stop it; there is no point in it, anyway!

MANHOLD: So what are we supposed to do now?

IRA: She is leaving and that's it. That's the way she wants it.

Manhold looks for wine and finds a halfway full carafe behind the sofa. He drinks from it, greedily, wine trickles down his shirt. Suddenly Manhold breaks out into long and loud screams.

MANHOLD: What are we heading for?

IRA: Manhold…

Ira embraces Manhold who breaks down crying. Ira caresses Manhold all over and keeps talking to him, soothingly and consoling. Manhold howls like a dog.

IRA: Life will go on, everything will go on, I know for sure. Things will be looking up again, everything will be uphill, and all the signs are there. It's only a question of time when you'll be up at the top again, all celebrated; and me, as always, by your side! That's the way it will be!

MANHOLD: Yes, Ira, why couldn't I grasp this, of course you are right, that's the way it will be and no different.

IRA: Uphill, uphill, that's how it will turn out; the crisis is a long way behind us!

MANHOLD: I'm so unhappy, Ira!

IRA: I know!

MANHOLD: Unhappier than you could ever imagine!

IRA: Me too. No flame burns as fast as that of a woman.

MANHOLD: The way you put it, it makes me shudder.

IRA: It's true, believe me.

MANHOLD: I will always love you.

IRA: Will you?

MANHOLD: Even if we lose everything, I will always love you.

IRA: There is a new day tomorrow!

MANHOLD: There is a new day tomorrow! And
                tomorrow things will be looking up
                again!

IRA: From tomorrow onwards things will
                be looking up, Manhold!

*Lyaman comes from the kitchen. Her face is tearstained, she is
still undressed.*

LYAMAN: I'll stay, after all.

Ira and Manhold, crouching on the floor, look at her.

LYMAN: I'm so alone in this world!

IRA: But you've got your home country!

LYAMAN: And yet, I'm so lonesome!

MANHOLD: Lyaman, you have no idea what it's like
                to be lonesome.

LYAMAN: I would like to stay, I wanted to leave
                because...

IRA: We don't believe you anymore...

MANHOLD: You've got to prove that you are
                serious about this.

LYAMAN:	How could I?
MANHOLD:	I don't really know.
IRA:	Let's dance.

The sound of Let It Loose *by the Rolling Stones can be heard. Ira, Manhold and Lyaman dance in a restrained way. Manhold breaks down again, crying. Ira casts herself on him; Lyaman embraces both.*

LYAMAN:	Everything will turn out well!
IRA:	Yes, all will turn out well!
MANHOLD:	Nothing will turn out well! I'm sick of hearing all this!
IRA:	Al will turn out well, things will be looking up, you'll see.
LYMAN:	We are friends!
MANHOLD:	There aren't any friends! Nowhere!
IRA:	Do you want to die then, Manhold?
MANHOLD:	I keep dying all the time.
LYAMAN:	We must will things to turn out well, and then they will.
MANHOLD:	How would you know!

IRA: Maybe she is right…

MANHOLD: Yes, perhaps she is right, but I don't believe it.

LYAMAN: You've hurt me so!

IRA: Nobody has hurt you.

LYAMAN: Hurt like no one ever has before!

MANHOLD: And you want to stay in such a place even if that is the case?

LYMAN: Yes, I want to stay in that place.

IRA: Yes, do stay!

MANHOLD: Do stay, Lyaman!

LYAMAN: I will stay!

IRA: So lonesome.

LYAMAN: So lonesome!

MANHOLD: Lonesome like nobody can imagine!

LYAMAN: But here I am, as your daughter and lover, your beloved daughter!

IRA: And now things will be looking up!

The three of them sit around on the floor, crying; Lyaman caresses the two.

END